WHEN MARRIAGE IS HARD

From Conflict to Connection

A guidebook from one who has been there.

JULIE BENDER

TABLE OF CONTENTS

Acknowledgments v

Dear Reader 1

My Story 3

Your Story 15

Problems to Face 21

Steps to Take 33

Finding Hope 65

Finding Your Hope 69

When Memories Return 71

Before You Go 75

The Hope We've Found 77

Beginning Faith 79

Battered Faith 85

Building Faith 91

About the Author 95

Resources 97

About Grit and Grace Life 99

Published in the U.S. by: The Grit and Grace Project
Address: P. O. Box 247
          Estero, FL 33929
Email: info@thegritandgraceproject.org
Web Address: www.gritandgracelife.com
Author: Julie Bender
Editor: Ashley Johnson
Special Projects Manager: Allison McCormick
Photo credits: All photos courtesy of Shutterstock and Unsplash

This book is written by the author to share her life experience with the sole purpose of providing insight, encouragement, and hope. The information provided in this book is for informational purposes only and is not intended to substitute professional counseling or treatment.

The Grit and Grace Project®
#gritandgracelife

ACKNOWLEDGMENTS

To Donny, you truly are the love of my life. I'm so grateful I get to spend my days learning to love you better. Thank you for all the ways you love, serve, and lead me and our children. May God continue to get glory from our story. In all ways, always.

To Darlene Brock, I am forever indebted to your belief in me. I'm privileged to call you a mentor and colleague but also a friend. Thank you for trusting that who I was when we met was just the beginning. I treasure all of the off-mic conversations we've had and I am so proud of all we have done together so far. I promise to always take the longer prompts in our videos and hug you a little longer than you can tolerate—as long as you keep giving me opportunities I'm slightly underqualified for and cheering me on as I navigate them. I hope D and I make it like you and Dan have, one day never admitting to how long we've been married but still living happily ever after through the ups and downs.

To Ashley Johnson, thank you for taking all my words, in person and in writing, and listening with care and invaluable insight. You are a true treasure, and I am so proud to know you and work together as long as God allows. I have a deep respect for you and greatly appreciate your contribution to this project and everything at The Grit and Grace Project.

DEAR READER

This book is almost 20 years in the making. At the young age of 22, I sought out a relatable marriage resource and couldn't find what I needed. So, now, I'm penning my own. Why? Because I know what it's like to wonder if your marriage is "normal," if you're normal, or... if maybe you just aren't quite cut out for wife-ing—at least, not to the degree of perfection you feel pressured to achieve.

This book is for the wife who loves her husband but struggles to like him sometimes. Who wants her marriage to thrive but finds her life is not as dreamy as her beloved Hallmark movies (or reality TV shows) claim it could—or should—be. For the wifey who knows there could be more for her marriage but is at a loss for practical ways to get there while also managing the rest of her life. I'm that wife, and I'm still figuring it out. But, I've learned some real steps to take and pitfalls to avoid, and I want you to start with the right steps and skip the bad ones so you can enjoy your man (and marriage) more—now.

So, "Hey girl, hey!" Let's get into it, for real.

Julie

"And now, dear brothers and sisters, one final thing. Fix your thoughts on what is true, and honorable, and right, and pure, and lovely, and admirable. Think about things that are excellent and worthy of praise."

—*Philippians 4:8*

MY STORY

I feel a need to tell you right away that I've been married twice. I was only 21 years old when I married my college sweetheart, and after 11.5 years, I became a widow unexpectedly. Then, I married the love of my life (whom I met on Match.com) when I was a single mom in my mid-30s.

The marriage advice I am offering, the problems I've faced, and the steps I suggest you take have been tested and tried with these two men, and I've seen them work (for the most part) with both. I am not sharing this so that you will simply take my word for it. Instead, I want you to understand that I've been married to two very different men, in two very different seasons of life, and those realities have taught me some foundational truths about marriage that I go back to over and over again while trying to invest in my marriage today.

To start, let's talk about that 21-year-old girl at the first altar.

Before we go there, I should tell you that my childhood was hard. You see, my mom was a teenager when I was born, and she wasn't able to raise me or my sisters. My dad was not in the picture either, actually, because he was in jail. I grew up in my great-grandmother's home, and it was very turbulent. I often told myself, "It could be worse, at least you're not on the streets or surrounded by drugs." I share this because, with time and healing, I've come to understand just how much my background impacted my decisions—including my choice to clearly ignore some serious red flags.

I was in college when I met Paul, my first husband. I was new to embracing my faith in every area of my life—beyond just going to church on Sunday. Paul pursued me pretty obviously, and even though I had "sworn off dating" for a time (because, as I was growing in my relationship with God, I realized how much my difficult childhood had messed with my ability to judge good character in guys), I said yes to *one date*. That way, I could let him down easy and explain my need for the dating hiatus.

All it took was a little attention from a guy for me to change my no-dating rule. Plus, Paul was a Christian, came from a home with still-married parents, and seemed like an all-around "good guy." I figured that since I wasn't incredibly attracted to him, our relationship would be safe and could actually help me grow. And it did, for a while. Soon, we were exclusive. I think I even dropped the "L word" first. Looking back, I see that I was simply trying to progress in the relationship; I wasn't in love, but I was pretty certain he was.

Our dating was kind of like that. We moved forward although I felt an inner sense that it wasn't right. I thought, "But he is a good guy, and we could have a healthy relationship." Having the right intentions is what matters, right?

I don't think I had any idea just how traumatized I was by my childhood. I didn't recognize the abandonment issues, my fear of not being loved and wanted, and constantly feeling like I was too much and not enough all at the same time. I didn't see how much I craved a man's attention because I never had a father in my life. I just knew I wanted to be married. I didn't realize I was settling because I desired any level of security. This was the scenario that led me to accept a proposal from Paul, knowing in my gut that our relationship had become truly unhealthy and codependent. (Do I even need to tell you that I didn't know that term?)

"Getting married will solve our problems," I thought. His anxiety would lessen when we could spend more time together. His workaholism (apparent even at 21) would settle down once we shared some expenses by living together. We would be married and having sex, so we'd have less shame over creeping close to the line that Christian purity culture taught us to avoid like the plague. I could help him with it all. And, I wouldn't have to worry about where to live because he could afford to buy us a condo. I was about to graduate college and leave my roommates, what else could I do?

So, with legitimate fear in my stomach (beyond wedding day jitters), I vowed to follow Paul as the leader of our home, to be his helpmate, and to love him in sickness and in health until death do us part. I had been taking care of myself my entire life. Now, I had someone who vowed to take care of me. And, I hoped it would all be fine because we both claimed to want a God-centered marriage.

But it wasn't fine. A few days later, I was crying on our honeymoon because Paul was anxious about being away from work and wanted to leave Jamaica early. He sent me to the front desk to find out if or we could get a partial refund if we left right then, and if so, how much. They said we had prepaid at booking, and whether we stayed or left, we'd pay the full amount—no refund. With that, he said we could stay, but there was true annoyance and zero joy in his tone. I knew right then we were in trouble. But he didn't seem all that fazed. It just... was what it was.

That's what it was like being married to Paul.

He focused on work. He truly believed his role as a husband was that of a provider and that he was accomplishing it. But he was not able to provide for me emotionally. Nor could he really provide for me spiritually, because he thought I expected too much.

I know that, in some ways, I did. I expected marriage to fix our problems, but marriage doesn't work that way. Two people must be in it, working on it, seeing and working on the weaknesses while developing the strengths. Weathering the trials together, growing in and through what life throws at you, because you're a team.

After one year of marriage, I was in the Christian living section of the bookstore looking for advice. I wanted more. I knew what the Bible taught about marriage, but I needed advice for when it didn't seem to be going that way. At times, Paul agreed that our marriage could be better, but he was way too overwhelmed with his anxiety and work to have the headspace to invest in it.

So, I figured I could do it. I found the book, *The Power of a Praying Wife*, and just knew it would fix him (us, whatever... same thing, right?).

Upon reading the first few pages, I was hit with the realization that God had so much to say to me as a wife, even if Paul wasn't willing to take notes or suggestions from me, open his Bible, or talk to anyone about the true state of our marriage. I could focus on my calling and seek to honor God in my marriage, which would have a positive effect.

And it did. I was faced with my own sin, apathy, and selfishness. I recognized I wanted him to do a lot of things, and I didn't seem to think I needed work. Such pride. Over the next couple of years, I devoted myself to changing the way I treated him, even though it didn't really change the way he treated me.

Is this encouraging yet?

Even though I didn't see him adopting the changes I hoped for, I felt more fulfilled than ever because I honestly knew what God was calling me to, and I knew I was doing my best even though I failed often. I had new pride in taking my role as Paul's wife very seriously, trusting that God saw my good work and was pleased with it. I prayed for him often and in detail. Paul and I didn't pray together, but that was okay. I knew that if I didn't pray for him, no one else would. Except maybe his mom. I sought to serve him in meaningful ways that mattered to him. He liked his back scratched. I praised his work ethic. I initiated sex regularly. I made his favorite foods. We got a dog, even though I really didn't want one. And then we got another, and I shouldered the work of caring for them both.

I noticed things were starting to get better. And he noticed, too, because I overheard him telling a friend that he had seen me putting more intention into our marriage, and he felt like I made a difference. Then, he started trying more, too. After about 7 years of marriage, we finally felt like we were in a good place and decided to try for a baby.

Lincoln was born right before our 8th anniversary, and we had our best year and a half after his birth. We enjoyed being parents. Lincoln loved Paul and wanted to be around him whenever he could. They loved to ride in his truck together and Linc became a real car guy under his influence. We dedicated Lincoln to the Lord at our church, moved to Paul's dream house, and loved our Friday pizza nights and Panera Saturday mornings.

Unfortunately, this season didn't last long for our family. Paul suffered a big setback after losing a friend to cancer. This sent him spiraling into a deep depression, and he started drinking heavily. I begged him to get some counseling to deal with the loss and the anxiety that was increasing as he tried to cope through working and drinking. He resented the insinuation that he needed help. Having been together nearly 15 years, I also knew that he had some unaddressed wounds from his childhood. I suggested he could talk about those while also dealing with his grief. Those struggles, plus the pressures of running his business, were truly wearing on him and, therefore, our marriage. It was becoming difficult to hide from Lincoln, too.

After a couple of months without improvement and seeing his drinking increase (plus some other details for another conversation), it became apparent that I needed to initiate a short-term separation.

The purpose was to express to Paul just how serious I was about him getting help to get out of his current desperate state.

I was emboldened by the need to protect Lincoln from growing up and thinking this behavior—denial and avoiding work on personal/spiritual problems while losing yourself in your career—was the way to go. It was what was modeled to Paul, and he was faithfully passing it on. But I wanted different. For all of us. I took Lincoln, and we found a place to stay for a three-month period while Paul and I worked individually on our spiritual and mental health. Then, we could begin to work as a couple to rebuild a healthy foundation in our marriage.

Two months into this, we had our first joint marriage counseling appointment. I was scared to share how I felt and the list of the areas I believed needed to be addressed and changed, but his counselor had requested I come up with clear guidelines for what I would need to feel ready to come home. In previous conversations like this over the years, I didn't feel safe sharing my needs because Paul was always under so much stress and pressure that I didn't want to add to his plate. I explained this in our session, and my husband told me with tears in his eyes that he wanted to hear so he could do the work to bring me home. We had a very hard conversation, and I shared several of my needs. I was not able to get to them all during that first session, but I felt encouraged that subsequent sessions would address them in time. Paul listened intently, and we set a time to meet again.

We left the appointment hand in hand, which was very rare. It had even been on my list (a point that I didn't get to mention) that he would initiate non-sexual touch.

We didn't say much, but we shared a knowing look, as couples who have been together for years can. Our look said that we had a lot of work to do, but with the right guidelines and both of us putting in the effort, we <u>can</u> do it. He left our session to go see our son, who was with Paul's mom, even though he had to wake up at 4 a.m. the next day. He wanted to take time to see Linc since it was "his day" under our current separation terms. These were all great signs that this transformation was real.

And then, everything changed.

The next day, I got an unimaginable call. Paul had fallen off a ladder, and I needed to come quickly. They rushed him into surgery for a serious head injury but said we'd have to wait to see if he responded well. The doctors advised his parents and me that if he survived, he'd have a long road to recovery and only time would tell.

As the doctor walked away, Paul's parents and I agreed that Paul would want to wake up, shocking the doctors with his recovery, or he would want to pass away, without feeling one more ounce of pain.

Four days later, after no improvement, the doctors explained he would stay indefinitely in his vegetative state, or, I could remove him from life support. Paul had told me once that he'd never want to live that way, so I did what I knew he'd want me to do. I told them we would let him go.

The night before I took him off life support, I brought a towel and a basin into his hospital room, and I washed his feet, thanking God for the opportunity to be Mrs. Paul Graham for 11.5 years. For the ways God used his life to shape and refine mine. For the privilege it was to hold his hand 'til death parted us the next day.

On that fateful morning, as I stood at his bedside and waited for his organs to fail, I held his hand while humming the melody of "Good Good Father." I told him repeatedly that he was loved, that I would take care of Lincoln, and that we were proud of him. And then he was gone.

I don't have the pages here to share about the grief of widowhood, but I was absolutely shocked by this turn of events. Everything felt so unfinished.

Days later, I honored my husband at his funeral by sharing what a good man he was and that he would no longer have to struggle in this life... that he was free, happy, and healthy in heaven. My son sat in the front row with much more understanding than you'd expect from a 3.5-year-old. When I first told Linc that his daddy had died, he wailed and cried, but within a few minutes he sniffled and asked if we could pray and ask God for a new daddy. Lord, have mercy. Well, I had learned to pray daily for my husband. It was time to do so again.

About two weeks later, my now-husband moved to our town. I wouldn't meet him for another year and a half, but God was lining it all up.

A Fateful FaceTime

When Donny and I met online, I had been dating for about a year. I had grown so much through therapy and recovery groups I attended during my separation and after Paul's death. I took inventory of what had gone wrong leading up to and throughout my marriage so that I could be healthier and wiser when choosing another partner.

My therapist and colleague at Grit and Grace Life, Dr. Zoe, helped me develop a detailed list of what I was looking for to prevent me from settling a second time. I was ready to choose someone not just for me but to be Lincoln's new daddy, too.

When I met D, I instantly knew he was "The One." It was like a Hallmark movie. After messaging on Match.com for a few days, I accidentally responded to his text message with a FaceTime video. I was wearing ZERO makeup, complete with wet hair and an oversized tee and leggings. I looked nothing like my dating app profile pictures. But we clicked immediately. We went on our first date two days later. We fell in love quickly, and he met Lincoln two weeks later on Father's Day.

Just over a year later, he surprised me with an incredibly sweet and thoughtful proposal. But first, he asked Lincoln if he could be his dad. A few months later, we wed, sharing deeply personal vows, promising to love one another for better or worse, and putting God at the center of our family. Donny had never been married, and I was getting my second chance at love. We were—are—both so grateful.

Time has passed since this season of our family's life, and it's beautiful to see the way our lives continue to merge. Like the addition of our beautiful daughter, Reverie. And how Donny has not only become a father to Lincoln, but he has made Lincoln a brother, too. (And he's a fabulous one.) Grace upon grace.

Now, here's the real marriage advice.

My marriage to Donny has had some of the same challenges I experienced with Paul. But, the way I approach them as a wife and the way he approaches them as a husband are very different. And that's what matters.

I went in-depth on my marriage to Paul because it shaped how I think about and behave in my marriage to Donny. I've lived 'til death do us part, and as I love D today, I recognize that at any point, I could lose him, too. That causes me to work harder to keep our marriage healthy. When we have a conflict, I get triggered by what I've endured before and am motivated to seek reconciliation faster for both of us and our kids.

My tender scars serve as reminders of what I'm willing to work for. And the effort is truly worth it.

"I don't know exactly what the future holds, but I'm stepping forward with grit, anchored in grace."

—Julie Bender

YOUR STORY

Now, it's time to write Your Story.

No two stories are the same. Even if we've faced similar challenges, we have nuances and circumstances unique to us. As you begin to take steps to strengthen your marriage, I want you to go back and think about your journey to date.

Tell your story here, even if you're the only one who ever reads it. There's purpose and healing in reflection like this.

"On the day I called, You answered me; and You made me bold and confident with [renewed] strength in my life."

—Psalm 138:3 AMP

PROBLEMS TO FACE

Marriage is a beautiful gift from a loving God. But let's be honest, it can be hard, too. When we say "I do," we have dreams and hopes of how it will be. Often, those hopes and dreams morph into expectations. And expectations can be like slow cracks spreading through your house, threatening the foundation of your marriage. As you live day to day as a wife, months stacking into years, you will undoubtedly encounter problems. I know I did, and I still do. In this section, I address some of the common struggles I think many marriages face.

First, I want you to be encouraged by acknowledging the fact that every marriage experiences problems. There is no perfect marriage, because there are no perfect people. When two sinners do life together, they are going to experience conflict due to each person's own selfishness, pride, and mishandling of emotions. And then, life will throw challenges at you that you can't avoid (and some you could have).

When we learn to accept and embrace the fact that marriage is going to challenge us, we can begin to face our problems with a better attitude and outcome.

Let's look at five common issues many marriages face.

Comparison

When D and I were dating, we used to go out all the time. Even after we tied the knot, we spent more time together than we do now. I loved how we prioritized it. Fast forward two years, and we have added a lot of responsibilities to our plate. So, date night happens maybe every 6-8 weeks.

I also see others around me who seem to date their spouse weekly. Many are taking couples' trips annually. But in my house, we are in a season where that's just not possible. Whether I'm looking at other couples around us or even back to "better times" within my own marriage, it's easy to fall into the comparison trap and feel discouraged.

You've heard it said, "Comparison is the thief of joy," and I can see how it has the potential to kill many marriages. The grass often looks greener in your neighbor's yard.

Other husbands seem better, and you see them everywhere—in your social media feed, on TV, standing at your pulpit, living down the street. You notice the husbands who are better at making money, co-parenting, communication, or even having fun. And suddenly, you're disappointed. I find myself comparing my husband of today to who he was as my boyfriend in our first months of dating. And he falls short.

Have you ever compared your husband or marriage to your past relationships or other people? If yes, what was the outcome of your comparison?

Growing Apart

There have been times in my marriage with Donny when I sensed us drifting apart. I've already confessed that our regular date nights have slipped since marrying. I also mentioned that we're actively choosing to invest in his business. We have two children in two different stages of life. And I'm nurturing my own career. All of these things take time and energy. So, sometimes we can feel like we're "not as close" simply because of the busy season of life we are in.

I try to be aware of this because I've heard other people share some of these reasons for wanting to throw in the towel: We just grew apart. We fell out of love. We were so young when we got married—we aren't the same people. He doesn't make me happy anymore.

When I step back from these statements, I can see how the loss of regular, intentional connection can lead to some of these bigger thoughts and feelings. It's not even tense or conflict-ridden. It's just not exciting anymore.

Have you ever felt like you and your husband are growing apart? Perhaps the intimacy you shared when first married has been replaced by busy schedules, demanding careers, and little ones to care for. Take time to think about your marriage and capture the changes you've noticed below.

High Conflict

The going gets tough, and you want to get going. If you've been married for a minute, you've likely been in a season where conflict seems to reign and your communication as a couple isn't working. Every "little thing" turns into a fight and the fight never really resolves.

Tension. Frustration. Miscommunication. Hurt. Eventually, apathy. (Which may have landed you in "we've grown apart" territory.)

Maybe you're like me and these times, stressful as they are, are made worse by the fact that you feel shame over the thoughts you're having about the hopelessness you feel. You're convinced it will never get better. "If I was a good wife, it wouldn't be this hard..." "I should never have gotten married..." "We won't make it through this..." Those are ripped straight from my thought life. When my husband and I are stuck in a conflict cycle, I quickly assume it's all my fault. And not just the current argument, but anything hard in our relationship must be something I'm doing wrong. I had one difficult marriage, it must be me. This literally happens *every* time we argue. Whether about dinner plans or raising our kids or if a bill got paid on time.

My husband tends to say things like, "It shouldn't be this hard," during seasons of frequent conflicts, compounding my fear of abandonment and insecurity over not being able to have a healthy marriage.

Conflict moves in and threatens to tear up the blueprint to the dream house you hoped your marriage and home would be. It's scenarios like this where you start to seriously consider how just giving up would be easier. But leaving won't fix it.

Forbes recently cited a statistic that stated the #1 reason for divorce was lack of commitment. [1] Are you committed to working on identifying the issues and finding ways to address them in your marriage? Consider why or why not. Is your husband willing to work on your marriage to improve it?

Self-Neglect

Because of my abandonment and rejection wounds from childhood, I am prone to feel unlovable. This spirals quickly into acting clingy and/or quick-tempered toward my spouse. Which triggers his flight reaction. Doesn't that sound fun? But I truly believe a lot of our cycles of struggle start from me neglecting to take care of myself.

The Bible says that we love because God first loved us (1 John 4:19). This should be especially true in marriage. We are meant to be a tangible expression of God's love to our spouse. But sometimes, there's a roadblock because we aren't secure in the love of God or we just don't love ourselves. If we don't see ourselves as worthy and deserving of love, we struggle to ask for it and/or to receive it. This will cause a marriage to gradually deteriorate (because one or both people are slowly dying on the inside).

As you read the text above, what immediately came to mind? Do you take time to care for your mental, emotional, and spiritual needs? Do you believe God loves you? Are there old wounds that keep you from fully loving God, yourself, and others?

Spiritual Differences

Life can feel very lonely when you're not viewing it through the same faith lens as your husband. Especially if, at some point, you did. This was such a hardship in my first marriage, and I guarantee this book wouldn't be in your hands if I hadn't felt this pain. I know how hard it is to want to grow in faith with your man, and he's not interested. It felt almost crazy at times.

So many marriages experience an imbalance when it comes to their spiritual life. Maybe you got married and then became a Christian and he did not (or vice versa). Sometimes this chasm comes after a life event outside of your control happens, and you both handle it differently. What pushes you to pursue God pushes him further away from God. Or, maybe there's always been a difference in your faith lives, but as you've continued to grow, so has the gap. And there's friction. Or apathy. And it's bothering you that he's not following along. Other times, he's the one growing and you're staying put thank-you-very-much.

As you think about you and your husband's spiritual walk, are you in sync, on different pages, or reading completely different books? Have you talked about where you're at? What is one step you can take to help address your differences?

"It's one thing to say 'I do' thinking about happily ever after... it's a choice to put in the effort to stay happy together."

—Julie Bender

STEPS TO TAKE

Marriage is a marathon, not a sprint. Maybe you haven't really thought about it, but the man you married has changed since you became his wife. And so have you. And that is okay. You're going to change even more. The trick is to grow with him.

I used to notice little changes in Donny and become fearful. "Oh no, he's different. He didn't do that before. Do I even know him anymore?" But one day it occurred to me that I recognized changes and I still saw the man I married. And something just clicked. I get to grow and change with this man. I thanked God right then and there that I was the one who got this view of him and asked for the Holy Spirit's guidance to help me maintain a right perspective. I'll see all the versions of him like no one else will. It's my privilege to do life next to him, learning how to love him in each season as we go. And he gets to do that with me. I've changed since I promised my heart to him, and he's committed to learning how to love me in the ways I need as I develop, too. What a gift. What a worthy cause.

To go the distance with this man you have to give yourself and him so much grace. You need to laugh through some of the problems you face without giving them too much weight. And you can tackle each problem with the desire to overcome it, together, becoming stronger with time.

With that vantage point, let's go back through each problem and consider practical steps to take.

Comparison Becomes Adoration

Earlier I said that I tend to compare my husband to who he was when we were dating and that he falls short. But here's the deal, if I am honest, so do I. Neither of us are able to be who we were back then, because, as I mentioned, life has changed.

Since we started dating, we've had another child. We are also in a season where my husband is building our business in order to sustain not only us but over a dozen employees. Our daughter is entering her toddler years, and we don't leave her with Lincoln's grandparents (my first husband's parents), so it's not as easy (read: affordable or convenient) to have regular dates. But, we have discussed this as a couple, and we both understand why we're making sacrifices in these years to allow for more freedom later. I'm not holding it against my husband. I am aware of the entire situation and trusting the outcome will be worth it. So, I choose to focus on us, not on how others are doing life.

One thing I have found to be very helpful in battling the comparison trap is to focus on what I have that is worthy of celebrating. In fact, I have committed the Bible verse below to memory, and I would encourage you to do the same. Put it somewhere that you can see it often, and let it be the lens through which you see your partner. Choose to view your marriage like this:

"And now, dear brothers and sisters, one final thing. Fix your thoughts on what is true, and honorable, and right, and pure, and lovely, and admirable. Think about things that are excellent and worthy of praise." —Philippians 4:8, NLT

I want to share another verse that has changed the way I show up in my marriage, but first I will say that I prefer to read it in its entire context because context matters. Without it, we can get into trouble pulling verses out and trying to apply them in ways that aren't God's intent. But, due to length, I'll have you look it up in your own Bible or do a quick Google search. The passage is 1 Peter 3:1-9. What we really need to focus on is in the first verse:

"Wives, in the same way submit yourselves to your own husbands so that, if any of them do not believe the word, they may be won over without words by the behavior of their wives..."

I want you to highlight the words "your own" in the first verse. Your own. Focusing on your own husband will help you to keep comparison from choking the life out of your marriage. Learn to look for the true, lovely, admirable things in him. Not constantly sizing him up to who you want him to be, who he could be, or who he was.

The way I loved Paul, with this verse directing my mindset, brought peace and purpose. When I apply it to my husband Donny, I smile at how it differs ever so slightly, but in some ways, remains the same. There are some parts of the role of a wife that are universal, but the Holy Spirit will tell you how you are to love your own husband day by day, season by season, circumstance by circumstance. How perfectly personal God and marriage are.

Last, I've found it helpful to consider the entertainment I'm consuming. Are there any television shows, movies, books, or social media accounts that negatively impact your perception of your marriage? You may want to reconsider these.

What are some ways comparison is threatening your marriage? What life stages and changes might be impacting your current situation? What are some ways God is showing you to love or serve your husband right now? What are some special things about him you can meditate on? What is admirable about your marriage and your husband? Write it all down.

When you're finished, consider taking this a step further. Call, text, or write him a note today telling him something you love or appreciate about him. Sow a seed in order to grow fruit in your marriage with one act of adoration.

Growing Apart Becomes
Intentional Connection

What I have come to understand is that people drift apart when they're not trying to stay connected. This is possible in any relationship, and it's inevitable. We cannot expect to stay close to someone if we don't make an effort to do so.

So, when I notice my husband and I drifting apart, I make an effort to combat it. Otherwise, I truly believe it will only get worse. I don't think it will simply auto-correct; I must become proactive. On my best days, I start fighting it before it happens. And, when it's already happening, I remind myself that it's not too late. I will not believe that lie.

Yes, it is true that my husband and I haven't been going on dates as much as we did when we were dating. But, I also had to admit to myself that I was waiting for him to initiate dates. And he's been way too busy to think about it. I know this, because I know him and the season we're in. So, instead of becoming bitter over it or comparing him to the guy in the romance novel I just finished, I can take action. I can set up the date night myself. I can arrange the babysitter, make a reservation, or scope out a cool experience to try.

I find that it also helps when I am intentional about protecting the energy and atmosphere of our dates. That means, I do my best to keep it light and fun. I try to mix it up. And, for the most part, I don't bring up heavy conversations. Resolving conflicts is for another time. We work on them during our "connection talks"—which I will discuss later. Dates are a time to be playful, to explore, to escape the pressures of your life, and to invest in your relationship.

We've also found that we get the most out of dates when they're regularly scheduled (so one bad or skipped date doesn't affect us as much). We prioritize and protect them from constantly getting bumped by other important events. And we intentionally include affection and intimacy (those two things look different for everyone).

There are other ways I've found to connect with my husband outside of dates, in our normal, daily life, and those are equally as valuable. For example, I try to take time every day to look him in the eyes and engage him in conversation. Do I know what is going on in his life? Do I ask him how his day was or how certain events went during his day? If I want him to engage with me in this way, isn't it helpful for me to model the kind of questions that make me feel cared for?

If you and your husband struggle to communicate, here's an idea: I've heard it said that couples who engage in conversations while doing something else (walking, riding in the car, etc.) have more success in connecting. It feels less serious or official. Sometimes sitting face-to-face can feel confrontational.

Being a connected couple takes more than going on regular dates. You will benefit from having shared interests, too. Is there a hobby you both have that you can enjoy together more often? Can you take a class together about a topic you are both interested in?

Christian couples can really benefit from being in a faith community together. This can look like joining a couples' small group or church ministry where you can attend gatherings outside of worship services together. Anytime we have been in a small group, our marriage is automatically better. When we've cut that, we've felt it. Participating in a group like this without your spouse is a huge benefit as well, because taking care of you is vital to a healthy marriage (we'll talk about that more in the step titled *Self-Neglect Becomes Real Love*).

The focus here is to have recreational activities you enjoy together, even if there are things you do for/with your partner that aren't your passion but you engage in them to give your spouse time for the thing they enjoy.

For example, my husband loves drag racing and has gotten our son into it. It's not my favorite thing. (Race track with a toddler? It's hard. And hot.) But, seeing my husband doing something he loves gives me glimpses of his fullest self. Swoon. Likewise, he watches *Wheel of Fortune* with me at least twice a week because I've decided I want to be on the show one day and he's down for that. We enjoy competing as we watch together, congratulating the winner in our house at the end of the episode.

Find a way to be in each other's lives where you find your enjoyment.

Growing Your Emotional Intimacy

In my first marriage, my best friend was not my husband. I never understood it when women said, "I married my best friend." Paul and I didn't share much. I never wanted to burden him because of his anxiety, depression, and workload. I'm convinced that this worked against us. If I had chosen to be vulnerable with him, he'd have the opportunity to know me and connect with me in a meaningful way.

I have a very close friendship with Donny. And there have been times when I've had a problem or issue I wanted to discuss but put it off because I knew he was buried with work. And when I finally hit a breaking point, falling apart emotionally, he was hurt that I hadn't come to him sooner. He wanted to be my friend and lover. When I finally shared my feelings, he got to love and comfort me. And that made him feel like my protector which boosts his pride and yes, even his ego, which attracts me to him even more as I see him meeting my needs. Connection. It's sexy.

Let your husband be your friend and lover.

If you're not sharing in this way now, at least start by sharing your struggles with your husband and your friend(s). As you begin to trust him, having regular connection talks (defined below), make an intentional effort to go to him first more often. Share openly. Ask him to share openly. Give space to each other as you figure out how to incorporate this more and more. Thank him for the effort he gives. Trust the process.

Exercises to grow closer emotionally:

- Have regular fun dates (see previous section).
- Have regular "connection talks." This is an intentional time where you set aside distractions and update each other on all areas of life —your feelings, burdens, stressors, etc. Start with every other week for an hour, and adjust as needed.
- Share your needs clearly and kindly, offering grace as he seeks to meet them.
- Listen open-mindedly as he shares his needs and work diligently to try to meet them.
- Share your secrets with your husband before your best friend.

Lastly, I want to encourage you with this verse as you seek to bridge the gap you're sensing in your relationship. In Revelation 2:4, Jesus says, "But I have this complaint against you. You don't love me or each other as you did at first!" Yes, he is talking about his followers leaving the initial devotion they had to him and their faith, but I invite you to apply this concept to both your relationship with God and your husband.

Think back to when you fell in love with your husband. How did you spend your time? What did you like to do together? How many of those things are you still doing regularly? If your answer is none, you've just discovered Step One in working toward connection.

Consider talking with your husband about what you can bring back into your relationship that will foster closeness and connection. Maybe it's even a shared hobby or interest.

Have you drifted from your partner? Do any of the sentiments above ring true? Have you had other thoughts or feelings you would add? How can you start connecting with your husband? What kind of conversations can you initiate? What kind of dates or activities might the two of you enjoy? How can you be proactive in making more time for your marriage? Journal your thoughts and ideas below.

High Conflict Becomes Better Communication

When Donny and I were first together, we didn't fight often. If we did, it was kind of big and ugly (we called it"passionate"), and then we talked it through after a cool-off period and recovered quickly. As time and our marriage went on, the pressures of life around us increased and we started to struggle with more frequent conflict.

The CFOR Tool

Eventually we had to reach out for help. We asked our pastor (and friend) to help us break the unhealthy cycle we had fallen into and were unable to stop on our own.

HINT: Step one is to recognize there's a problem and you need to try something NEW.

Our pastor and his wife sat with us for a couple of hours while we aired our dirty laundry. We discussed some of the problems we were facing as a couple. He then introduced us to his CFOR tool for disputes, outlining four steps to work through when we face a conflict (See the printable resource QR code in the back).

At times we struggled to recognize when we should use CFOR. We would be well into a conflict that could have been minimized, but both of us were being too prideful to suggest we try the tool.

However, when we did, it helped us work through the dispute in a calmer, quicker, and more respectful way.

Here it is:
- C - Challenge. What challenges are you and your spouse facing? This could include concerns, worries, crimes (sins) and critiques.
- F - Feeling. What emotions are you and your spouse experiencing? Maybe you feel glad, sad, hurt, lonely, fearful, ashamed, guilty or angry.
- O - Own. What actions or behaviors do you or your spouse need to own up to? Address where you are each culpable.
- R - Reconciliation. How can you and your spouse remedy or restore the situation? How can you both plan to move forward?

I'll share a sample of a conflict from my marriage and then explain how we could apply the tool.

My husband and I are trying to buy our first home together. So exciting! And also, a little overwhelming and stressful.

I was (C) concerned with the pace at which we were pursuing one specific property and needed to talk to Donny about my (F) feelings.

I didn't do it well. I was leading with my fears and he perceived me as being negative. I shut down. I started thinking he thought I was stupid, or worse, that he would make decisions without me and I would lose my voice. So, I said things I shouldn't have.

I should have (O) owned the fact that I was struggling with some feelings that I hadn't shared and set up the conversation that way from the beginning. I needed to lead with vulnerability so he could hear that I wanted to share this not to put distance between us, but to bring us closer on an important decision.

For the (R) remedy, I had to apologize for not clearly communicating my needs in a way that I knew (from doing life with him, I know how he takes negativity) would keep him from getting defensive.

He needed to (O) own that he quickly went into defense mode.

We (R) restored unity by discussing it all again. We reiterated that we desire to find a home that we can both feel comfortable and excited about purchasing and reinforced the importance of sharing our thoughts and feelings with each other first throughout this process (not the agent, our kids, friends, etc.). Then we spent some time dreaming together about what our future will look like in whatever home God gives us.

It takes some practice, but with intention and repetition, you can avoid or recover more quickly from conflict by using CFOR.

Needs Assessment

In addition to handling conflict as it arises, I suggest you begin to attack known problems within your marriage with intentionality. You probably have a few issues you seem to circle back to that become repeat fights or points of frustration. I think, on some level, they will always be there, but your attitude toward them and your plan to face them can truly minimize their power to have a negative effect on your relationship.

Do you already know what some of these pitfalls are? Do you think your husband would cite the same ones or would he add anything? No matter what the pain points are, I have another tool to address them, and I'm really excited about it!

After having the conversation with our pastor and his wife, they continued to check in with us often. They knew we needed more than a tool for conflict. We needed to start digging into the deeper issues. When they asked me what I thought the problems were, my answers were different from Donny's. I couldn't believe what he chose to bring up, and vice versa. I talked about differing views on parenting and he shared frustration with my lack of excitement about taking a bigger role in our business.

But that was valuable insight. Instead of operating as though my pain points were more important than his, we could work through them all, in time. With a plan.

First, our pastor had us use the Needs Assessment for a few weeks (find it in the resource section). It outlines 10 common emotional needs in a marriage, and asks each partner to select their current top two. Then, you share those with one another and come up with three ways you will intentionally try to meet those two needs over the next week.

I loved this!

As I read through the problems, I could see how many of them were good areas to focus on in our marriage, but it was literally impossible to face them all at once. We each chose two. I found myself surprised at the two he selected, different from mine. (Can you see how conflict arises all over the place in marriage?)

But, the relief! If we hadn't had that conversation, I might have zeroed in on intentional ways of showing him love and affection tied to the needs I assumed he had, not the ones he was prioritizing in this season. But because he clearly told me where he wanted me to focus, it was my job then to just work on those things. And he with me.

We have found this tool to be very effective. Of course, over time, your priority of needs changes. Discuss that with your partner. Incorporate the Needs Assessment into your connection talks with your husband once a month and see how it helps chip away at those pesky problems, buried beneath the foundation of your marriage while using the CFOR as conflicts arise in everyday life.

Bonus Tip

Bonus tip for wives like me: Talk less. Listen more.

I throw this in because I know so many issues in my marriage could be helped by remembering this suggestion, sooner rather than later. Sometimes I need to just shut up, pray, take a moment (or a night), and come back to a conversation later. Do you need to try my bonus tip?

Something to Consider

I can't end this section without asking you to consider honestly if these tools and the commitment you both have to work on your marriage are "enough" right now or if you need to get outside help. There is no shame in seeking help. When you're facing a medical issue, you see a doctor. When you want to get fit, you hire a trainer or follow a plan. If you struggle to manage money, it's normal to hire a financial adviser. You get the picture. Your marriage is the most important relationship in your life. Asking for help by doing couples therapy or counseling, or, at the very least, taking a marriage class or joining a group is a wise investment in the health of your marriage and home.

I also suggest you look for and celebrate (like crazy) the small wins you have along the way. If he's willing to look at these tools, celebrate that. Even if you struggle to implement them, acknowledge the steps taken and let it breed hope in the outcome. When he hears a need and makes any step to meet it, celebrate that. After successfully using CFOR or seeing my husband do something I specifically asked him to do, I write him a note and leave it in his lunch box.

What do you need to celebrate right now about your husband's effort in addressing your marriage problems? I think far too often we forget to infuse joy and gratitude into our relationship. Praising him and letting him appreciate you can be a much-needed boost. And hint: you might need to tell him you need that. After the kids go to bed, at least once a week, I try to take my husband's face in my hands (pulling it away from his evening work) to tell him how thankful I am for all the ways he's trying to be a better husband and dad. He's not perfect. But he's trying to get better. And so am I.

A long time ago I came to the conclusion that marriage is not 50/50. No. Marriage is 100/100.

You've heard it said and have probably said it yourself: marriage only works when you both give 50%. But that breaks down because inevitably there will come a time when your spouse gives less than that (or worse, you perceive they're giving less), so then you give less, and you start growing apart, inch by inch. Mile by mile. The molehills that you let build into mountains threaten to crash into the dream home you thought your marriage was going to be when you said "yes." But, if you address the cracks as you see them—get your hammers out and do the DIY of assessing needs and repair leaks as you go—your dream home marriage has great potential.

So, no, marriage is not about you giving 50%. It's about you giving 100% and trusting God that your spouse is going to give 100% too. It's about choosing to give all of yourself to that man. You vowed it. So you do it.

How do you feel about making a plan to work on your marriage? Are you willing to try out the tools I mentioned? Record your thoughts and feelings below. Consider making a plan to bring these ideas up with your husband.

Self-Neglect Becomes Real Love

When I fail to take time to make sure I am "okay"—doing things I love, prioritizing rest, and working through negative thought patterns that might be cropping up—my marriage feels it. And fast.

You've heard the phrase, "You can't pour from an empty cup." The extreme version that applies to this sentiment is, "Put on your own oxygen mask before helping others."

Self-care feeds self-love which leads to self-growth. And happy, healthy marriages exist between people who recognize the importance of those things for each partner individually. The most fulfilling relationships are between two people who give and receive love from a healthy place. We can show up lovingly in our marriage when we understand and embrace God's love for us and our call to love others out of that security.

However, many women often think their best contribution to their family is to be the doting wife (and mom) who meets everyone's needs without a thought to her own.

This is one of the biggest errors I made in my first marriage, putting excess effort into trying to make my husband's life easier —essentially bearing some of his burdens while letting my mental, physical, and emotional health decline. It didn't serve either of us in the end; it hurt us both.

Let's look at what Jesus says in Matthew 22:37-40, MSG:

Jesus said, "Love the Lord your God with all your passion and prayer and intelligence.' This is the most important, the first on any list. But there is a second to set alongside it: 'Love others as well as you love yourself.' These two commands are pegs; everything in God's Law and the Prophets hangs from them."

I would like to challenge us to consider that our most important neighbor is our husband, and we are called to love our neighbor as we love ourselves. In this text, Jesus is assuming the hearer loves himself and is endeavoring to love his neighbor as well.

We invest in our marriages by taking good care of ourselves and showing attention and priority to our health and well-being physically, emotionally, and spiritually. When we are operating from this well-rounded wholeness, we have the best chance at harmony and happiness in our home.

At times, I've felt shame over taking time to do things that lighten my mood, countenance, and the pressure I feel, but I can't deny that when I let the guilt go, everything else feels better.

There have been countless times when just grabbing coffee with a friend, going for a walk by myself, or getting my nails done has lifted enough stress to help me feel filled up and ready to serve Donny with a happier countenance. He gets a joyful wife, not a dutiful one. He can tell the difference.

Here are some suggestions on how to put this into practice:

- Read for fun
- Do exercise you enjoy
- Practice times of solitude
- Enjoy time with friends who bring positive energy into your life
- Journal
- Therapy and/or counseling
- Take naps
- Take baths
- Participate in a Bible study group

Healthy wives lovingly encourage their husbands to do the same.

"It's not selfish to love yourself, take care of yourself, and to make your happiness a priority. It's necessary."—Mandy Hale

Do you struggle to love and care for yourself first so that you can better love and care for your husband and family? What issues has this caused in your emotional, physical, and/or spiritual health? Does your husband care for himself? Do you see how taking self-care more seriously will improve your health and your marriage? What are you doing right now to take care of yourself physically, emotionally, and spiritually? What do you need to change? To start or stop doing?

Spiritual Differences Become Spiritual Growth

About two years into my first marriage, I found myself swimming in disappointment, unmet expectations, frustration, and downright fear of the future never getting any better. I had married a Christian from a Christian home, but my home didn't feel like it was being built on a godly foundation. Our shared faith didn't feel shared.

I tried to point it out. I tried to talk about it. A lot. I asked him to read the Bible with me. To go to small groups together (we had done these things before; why couldn't we do them again?).

Hear me. It was right for me to ask for these things. If you desire them it's right for you too. But your tone, timing, and trust in God are everything.

I shared my concerns, but my husband wasn't interested in addressing this issue. I was pushing him away. It became clear (to him first!) that my sharing had become nagging. Even my beloved Bible clearly stated how that worked:

"It is better to live in a desert land than with a contentious and irritating woman." —Proverbs 21:19, NASB

And remember how I suggested you learn this one?

"And now let me speak to the wives. Be devoted to your own husbands, so that even if some of them do not obey the Word of God, your kind conduct may win them over without you saying a thing. For when they observe your pure, godly life before God, it will impact them deeply." —1 Peter 3:1-2, The Passion Translation

I knew in my gut that I was turning my husband off. I needed to find another way.

Pray for Your Husband

I sought counsel from wise women around me who encouraged me to pray. I agreed this was a good idea, but I didn't know what else to pray except "God, change him!" ... and I see it now, that was so proud.

Thankfully, I found a great book that put words and prayers to the issues I was (and still am) dealing with as a wife, and I developed the habit of praying more than I grumbled. More than I nagged. More than I allowed bitterness to build up. The book I found was *The Power of a Praying Wife* by Stormie O'Martian.

I encourage you to grab that book, but even if you don't, I can promise you that committing intentional time to pray specifically and consistently for your husband and marriage will bear much fruit.

Now, keeping it real—in my marriage today, where Donny and I both pursue God in a much more balanced way—I still grumble, nag, and get bitter, but markedly less, because I've learned from personal experience that prayer is my most effective marriage tool.

Here are some of the areas I suggest you pray for often: his work, his finances, his sexuality, his choices, his temptations, his priorities, his purpose, his health, his fears, his fatherhood, his past, his future, his emotions, and his marriage. Scan the QR code in the resources section at the back of the book for a more exhaustive list.

.

Because I recognized how crucial this practice was and I also realized that some wives might struggle with how to pray fervently for their men and marriage, I created a series called *#prayingforyourhusbanddaily*. I have dozens of videos, a few podcast episodes, and some articles with content specific to this important tool that I think can bless your husband and your marriage while also growing your relationship with God. You can also find these within the resources section.

Pray for His Wife

I left this one out of the list above because I wanted to unpack it. When I first found *The Power of a Praying Wife*, I was assaulted by the first chapter. The author dared to suggest that your husband might most benefit from a more humble, gentle, and godly wife.

Yikes. She was right.

Both of my husbands have needed that. I cannot pray for anything in his life to be "changed" (read: improved) unless I'm willing to first submit myself to God and ask him to do that same work in me.

Now, I want to offer you my biggest insight for dealing with this overall issue. When I focus on the things I wish he would do, the problem worsens. When, instead, I follow Jesus' model in Scripture, I find peace instantly.

"Why do you focus on the flaw in someone else's life and fail to notice the glaring flaws of your own life? How could you say to your friend, 'Here, let me show you where you're wrong,' when you are guilty of even more than he? You are overly critical, splitting hairs and being a hypocrite! You must acknowledge your own blind spots and deal with them before you will be able to deal with the blind spot of your friend." —Luke 6:41-42, TPT

God lovingly invited me to invest in the spiritual health of my hard marriage by investing firstly and fervently in my relationship with him. In doing so, I had perfectly tailored insight from the Holy Spirit on how to love my own husband in each season and circumstance. Did I always obey? No. I don't want to add "liar" to my lousy wife title here. But when I listened and obeyed, I found peace and purpose in loving God by loving the man with whom he had placed me in a covenant.

I remember God highlighting the idea of "three tries" to me with Paul. I could talk to him about an issue or need three times. After that, I'd be full-blown nagging. I was in pray-only territory if my husband showed no interest in working on that thing together.

But if your husband engages in conversation with you about it, it's open to discussion as needed.

I know you might be in a situation where talks of God and faith are downright hostile. I have been there. This is such a nuanced situation. I encourage you to surround yourself with healthy, godly people with whom you can be honest about your issues. I want you to be free to pursue God about this painful struggle, and I want you to have people you can lean on for encouragement, prayer, and fellowship. You need both. Even if your husband doesn't support it. Your spiritual health must be protected.

I suggest being a part of a faith community for corporate worship, Bible study, and connection with other godly wives. Even if he doesn't support it, you do it for you and your relationship with God, and ultimately, for your marriage.

Learn More about You and Your Husband

For your own health, I encourage you to learn more about yourself and your husband. When I was in the darkest days of my first marriage, I began to understand how much of my childhood trauma was truly unaddressed. I believed that because I was now walking with God, my hurts couldn't affect me anymore. But that wasn't true, because I hadn't really dealt with them. I was putting a Jesus Band-Aid on them.

I began seeking counseling, therapy, guided prayer sessions, and recovery groups to help me understand how my trauma affected me and my marriage. In doing so, I realized there was also unaddressed trauma my husband harbored that he hadn't dealt with. Uncovering this concept gave me more grace for him. And more to pray about.

In my marriage today, I still get triggered by life experiences that drudge up past pain and lies I can still believe at times. When I spiral, it can affect my relationship with my beloved husband. But, because of the work I have done, the foundation is there for me to find my footing more quickly. When I choose to speak truths over my fears or hurts, my marriage can ride those waves.

Because I know Donny intimately, I know things he's faced that can trip him up. When he's triggered and lashes out, I can see when it's not about me but about those hard things, and we can seek God together. I can at least pray insightfully and give him space to feel and process his emotions.

What I'm saying here is that growing your own relationship with God and processing your life's struggles in a healthy way will pay dividends into your marriage whether he does the same or not.

One Final Note

God never promised that your husband would "complete you." That's a line from a movie. God designed marriage to be a covenant that reflects his love for us and you are right to desire a spiritually strong, God-centered marriage. But rest in the truth that even if that is not your reality, God sees you and is even more loving than the most devoted husband you could ever imagine.

I was recently watching the TV series *The Chosen*. Simon's wife, Eden —expressing her frustration and disagreement with his decision to fish on the Sabbath—said to him, "God is with me even if you aren't." Mic drop, Eden.

Lean into your position as God's beloved one, dear friend.

What is the spiritual temperature of your marriage? What is God saying to you about your own husband and marriage right now? How can you pray for your husband? Have you tried any of the methods I mentioned above? Take all your honest fears and needs that your husband isn't meeting to God. He can handle it. What are you doing (or what can you do) to protect your spiritual health while in an imbalanced marriage? Do you have areas where you need deeper healing? Does he? How will you begin to address yours while offering grace for his? Would each of you be open to looking at these with a trusted professional or friend? Record your reflections, observations, and desires below.

"There are some parts of the role of a wife that are universal, but the Holy Spirit will tell you how you are to love your own husband day by day, season by season, circumstance by circumstance. How perfectly personal God and marriage are."

—Julie Bender

FINDING HOPE

What gives me the greatest hope in seeking a happy, thriving marriage is knowing that it is God's desire and design for me.

I can't look around at the world, pop culture, or even my peers and expect to find the answers to my problems. Most don't have the patience or the appetite for it. And that's not meant to be a judgment, but instead just an honest lens to look through.

As I've sought to learn from my first marriage, heal from my widowhood, and embrace my remarriage with intention and passion, the help I need comes from God.

When I doubt, I can pray.

When I'm mad, I can pray.

When I'm confused, I can turn to the Word and the countless passages about marriage and about loving Jesus and living like him. I get to seek insight from the Holy Spirit on how to proceed with my own husband.

And when I fail, I can ask God and my husband for forgiveness.

Notice, that's just what I can do. Me. That's my 100% contribution.

And when my husband adds in his, we're on our way.

A few steps forward, often, one step back. At least, that's how it seems to go in our house.

I want to leave a prayer here that you can turn to often.

Share it with him, if he's willing. But even if he's not, sow this seed into the garden of your marriage.

Dear God,

Thank you for the gift of marriage. I recognize that in this relationship, I get a glimpse of your love for me, and I have the honor of showering that onto my husband as well. Forgive me when I forget that beautiful correlation.

I pray for protection and covering over our covenant. We desire to glorify you in our marriage, but at times we fail miserably. Help us to extend grace to one another and even to ourselves in those times.

Help us to remain committed to intentional connection, open communication, passionate intimacy, healthy conflict resolution, and self-care that will keep us from drifting apart.

Protect us from the temptation to look outside of our marriage for the fulfillment of what is meant to come from one another. Also, protect us from seeking our ultimate fulfillment from one another, which is only available in our relationship with you.

As time goes by, draw us closer to one another and to you.

Allow us to grow in oneness over the years, becoming more in sync and more committed to this privilege of doing life together.

Allow the trials we inevitably experience as a couple to strengthen us and not tear us apart. Keep us committed to believing the best about each other and offering grace freely.

We're entrusting our covenant to you, the covenant-keeping God. Enable us through your Holy Spirit to see our marriage become more and more the way you designed it to be.

We love you and ask you to be the center of our marriage today and until death do us part.

Amen.

"A happy marriage is the union of two good forgivers."

—Ruth Bell Graham

FINDING YOUR HOPE

On the lines below, take inventory of any areas where your faith feels weak and record any opportunities you see for growth. Consider writing a prayer to God for his help, perspective, and strength.

WHEN MEMORIES RETURN

Even if you apply every step and suggestion I've written here, you will still face hard seasons in your marriage.

You will question if you can make it. I still do, and I wrote this book!

But. When you have those days (weeks, months, years) I encourage you to revisit the steps tested here and the journal that this book has become to help you face it head-on—with hope and a plan.

Remember, we expect the challenges, so they don't surprise us.

The beauty of living life with one person, building together through good and hard times, is that each problem you face and overcome serves as a building block—proof of what you can achieve together.

When my first husband died, I lost my chance at spending my whole life with one man. I had to grieve that.

But when I married Donny, I got the gift of living the rest of mine with him. He's my second chance and my true love. Sometimes I catch myself marveling at the fact that even though I didn't get to do some of my "growing up and growing old" with him, we have the rest of our lives to figure each other out. And that sounds exciting.

And on days when it sounds impossible, I ask God to give me the right perspective. The one where I remember that he is with us, he will show us the way, and he's not done with either one of us yet. There is still time. There is more grace. There is more learning, individually and as a couple. There's more forgiveness and more gratitude to be shared. There's more.

And there's beauty in working for more. You have more to celebrate when you've worked for it.

So, when you find yourself in a familiar conflict cycle don't lose heart. Double down and work it through. (Remember to use CFOR!)

What's on the other side of another victory with him will be another beautiful wreath to hang on the front door of that dream home you're building together.

And don't forget, it's always a good idea to reach out for help in building this marriage. It's never too late. It's not too early. Generations will be blessed by your humble pursuit of a strong marriage, and even strong marriages have hard chapters.

I keep coming back to this passage where Jesus is talking about loving our enemies. Stick with me. I'm not saying your husband is (or should be considered) your enemy. But the way we're instructed to love our foes when we love Jesus is counter-cultural. Shouldn't I be committed more emphatically to this kind of love for the man to whom I've covenanted my life?

I should have a covenant-over-convenience mentality, and this passage reminds me of the very bare minimum my husband can expect from his bride.

Love Your Enemies

"But I say to you who hear, love your enemies and do something wonderful for them in return for their hatred. When someone curses you, bless that person in return. When others mistreat and harass you, accept it as your mission to pray for them. To those who despise you, continue to serve them and minister to them. If someone takes away your coat, give him as a gift your shirt as well. When someone comes to beg from you, give to that person what you have. When things are wrongly taken from you, do not demand they be given back. The way you want others to treat you is how you should treat everyone else. Are you really showing true love by loving only those who love you? Even those who don't know God will do that. Are you really showing compassion when you do good deeds only to those who do good deeds to you? Even those who don't know God will do that."
—Luke 6:27-33, TPT

When the hard seasons return, love this way. Pray, pause, listen, forgive, talk, and listen more. Love some more. You can do this.

"*Marriage isn't 50/50. It's 100/100.*"

—Julie Bender

BEFORE YOU GO

I'm so proud of you. You committed to taking steps to strengthen your marriage. You're hopeful. You're prayerful. You should be proud, too. In this format, I can't address every common problem in marriage. I haven't even addressed all of the problems I know exist in mine, but take heart, God knows your heart and your husband's. He is with you. He is still writing your love story.

Maybe you did a "sand ceremony" at your wedding. I'm trusting that at the very least, you've seen one performed. The idea is that a bride and groom take two vases of two different colors of sand, representing each person, and combine them into one, symbolizing this new oneness initiated on your wedding day. Never again will each individual color be able to be separated from the other. You know how hard it is to get sand out of anything, try separating different colors of it from a jar! That's how your marriage is supposed to be. You're in it, purposefully intertwined, being built into a custom design that only the two of you could create. You are one; you're a team. Protect your oneness. Cherish it. Invest in it and believe the best for it. And thank God for it.

To the wifey who is fighting without her husband's participation —remember, you are not alone, even when it might feel like it. God is fighting for and with you. He sees you even when your husband does not. Take comfort and confidence in that truth. This is your reminder to make sure you take care of yourself as you keep entrusting your marriage to God.

You can do this, friend. I'm praying for you,

Julie

THE HOPE
WE'VE FOUND

This guidebook is a reminder that every woman's life is a journey. Every one of us will face good times and hard times. We all have stories that we love to tell and stories that still hurt to remember. While our human experiences may have similarities, there is no one who truly understands what you have been through and who you are better than Jesus. And he wants to invite you further into another journey—a faith journey—with him.

If you are searching and encountering him for the first time, we trust you will meet the Savior who gave all through the most difficult times because he had his love set on you. If you already know him and are building your relationship with him, we believe he will sustain you. If you have felt disheartened by the despair life can bring, we want you to know that God is not disappointed in your doubts or struggles—but is only more drawn to you in his tender mercy.

No matter where you are in your faith, God wants to meet you there. To be your hope and help. And we want you to know that he truly will.

Heather Jonsson, one of the Grit and Grace Life team writers, has unpacked each step of our faith journey: beginning faith, battered faith, and building faith. They are all a part of the faith journey the writers at Grit and Grace Life are on.

We hope that her written invitations will help you join us on this path that leads to a sense of purpose in this life and holds promise for the one to come.

Also, if you enjoy Heather's writing, we encourage you to find more of her personal work at www.heatherjjonsson.com.

BEGINNING FAITH

I wish you were sitting with me today, here in my living room. Here where the gentle spring winds play with my blue curtains, and the warm sun is melting away the frost of winter. There is a shift in the air.

You and I would take a walk, shedding our coats to allow the sun to kiss our skin. And we would sit outside on the patio, charmed by the green shoots pushing their way through the cold earth, which just last week was blanketed in snow. And I would look in your eyes and tell you, this awakening to life we feel, when what was dead begins to awaken, this is what has happened to my soul as I have come to know Jesus.

Have you ever had a friend who, just by spending an afternoon with them, makes you a better person—happy, full, content? So it is with Jesus. He loves you with an unstoppable, unchanging, perfect love, and his love changes you. This is the beauty of following Jesus. Like the daffodils which, against all odds, burst bright and yellow against a dreary backdrop of spring, this is the perfect work of Jesus' love for you.

Let me offer you a personal example. As a young mother with two small children, I was often angry when my husband had to work late. He isn't a workaholic, but sometimes he couldn't help but have a late evening completing his assigned tasks. When he finally arrived home I would give him the silent treatment, making sure he understood my anger by my cold shoulder. But I began to realize this was helping no one, and especially not myself as my anger grew like a weed, choking out the joy.

So I decided to use those extra hours talking with Jesus. I would share my frustration and ask for strength in my parenting. I looked for happy moments playing with my small children, and prayed for a patient, loving heart when my husband returned. Slowly, I changed. I became less of an angry wife when my husband walked in the door, and more joyful, happy, patient, and kind in my communication. This is the beauty of following Jesus. It changes us.

Like me, do you find yourself in need of the one who loves like no other? The one whose love changes you for the better? Now understand, following Jesus is not the easy life, ridding you of all difficulties; no matter our journey, the pain of life never fails to sting. However, following Jesus is a deeply fulfilling and rich life in the middle of both the beautiful and the broken.

God's Word tells us that we are needy, and he is limitless. We are broken, and he is the healer. We are deficient, and he is perfect. When we come to fully realize our insufficiency, we can truly see he is what we need.

If I'm honest, I'm still deeply needy and broken and deficient, and there is not a day that passes where I do not reach out asking Jesus to help me. But after years of following Jesus I am less broken and less deficient; now I am more whole, stronger, and at peace with myself and others. Jesus' love has cocooned me and changed me from who I was into who he created me to be; it is a process not a potion.

Dear one, is there something holding you back from following Jesus? Please journal your thoughts below.

After that, grab your Bible and look up John 10:10. No worries if you don't have a Bible; just do a quick google search to find it. Consider the life Jesus is freely offering you.

A checklist does not define those who follow Jesus, nor does obedience to a list of rules. Instead, following Jesus cultivates within your heart a blossoming garden, one full of flourishing in a fruitful relationship. A garden tucked away in your soul which even the most fierce of storms cannot destroy.

Here are some comforting realities about what it means to follow Jesus, straight from the Bible:

- "Every person who has walked this earth needs Jesus; he loves us exactly where we are and died for us when we didn't even know he cared. But God showed his great love for us by sending Christ to die for us while we were still sinners" (Romans 5:8, NLT).

- "For he has rescued us from the kingdom of darkness and transferred us into the Kingdom of his dear Son, who purchased our freedom and forgave our sins" (Colossians 1:13-14, NLT).

- "I pray that God, the source of hope, will fill you completely with joy and peace because you trust in him. Then you will overflow with confident hope through the power of the Holy Spirit" (Romans 15:13, NLT).

If you have never said, "Jesus, I want to follow you," then let me invite you to pray these words with me. "Jesus, you alone are the way, the truth, and the life. I believe you died for my sins so I can live. I trust you and I will follow you all the days of my life."

Welcome to new life, dear one! As followers of Jesus, we want to soak up as much sunlight as possible so we can flourish. There are so many ways you can do this, but let me lay out a few steps for you:

- Spend time reading or listening to God's Word. Set a time of the day, and let this habit become a rhythm in your daily life. The timing of this will ebb and flow with different seasons of life, so be mindful that this is a rhythm, not a rule.

- There are many wonderful Bible studies you can purchase, or you can read a few chapters of the Bible every day. I recommend you begin with the book of John, then move to Ephesians. John will teach you so much about Jesus, and Ephesians will teach you so much about Jesus in you. This is a beautiful combination.

What is one step you can take to begin your journey of faith?

BATTERED FAITH

One summer afternoon cloaked in sunshine, my friend and I walked under a brilliant sky that betrayed her dark emotions. In deep grief she turned to me and asked me, "Will I ever trust God again?" You see, together we had prayed and believed God for a pertinent need, only to have her life crumble around her. I scoured my heart for a wise response and came up empty.

Looking back, I wish someone would have told me that trust is much more challenging than one originally anticipates. I wish someone would have said, "Heather, trust will take more courage than you ever imagine." And most importantly, I wish someone would have reassured me that even shaky trust is still trust, like a child learning to walk.

In this season of life, the Psalms became dear to me. The psalmists who spoke in gut-wrenching honesty about their feelings towards God resonated with me. The Psalms they wrote that expressed these emotions are called laments. A lament is defined as a "passionate expression of grief or sorrow." We see them throughout scripture, as they were a way for God's people to bring their complaints before his throne.

There is no formula to a lament, no right or wrong answers. But a general outline looks like this:

- Expression of complaints, grievances, and pain
- Request for God to act
- Statement of surrender and trust because of who God is

Why don't you use the outline above and take some time to write a lament? (If you would like some examples, you can find laments in Psalm 3, 7, 13, 30, 88, 79, 137.)

Lamenting is one way to walk towards healing. Another way, especially when our faith feels feeble, is to swim back upstream and find the ocean where our faith began. We see this evident in Naomi's story found in the book of Ruth, which begins as one big detour of disappointment. Why don't you take time now to read the beginning of Naomi's story in Ruth 1:1-22.

In reading this story, we see that due to a famine, Naomi, her husband, and their two sons, left Bethlehem and moved to the country of Moab. But Naomi's husband died, leaving her alone with her sons. Then, after her two sons married, her sons also died. In lament, Naomi returned to Bethlehem with her foreign daughter-in-law, telling the people of her town, "Do not call me Naomi; call me Mara (meaning bitter), for the Almighty has dealt very bitterly with me. I went away full, and the Lord has brought me back empty."

Yet Naomi did an interesting thing. She trusted Boaz, her family's kinsman redeemer, and placed her future in his hands. The roles of a kinsman redeemer are laid out in the Levitical Law (Leviticus 25). In summary, a kinsman redeemer is a family relative who helps a weaker relative in need, or who willingly pays off the debts of a relative—essentially buying back what was lost due to the debt. From the time Naomi returned to Bethlehem, she knew that Boaz was their close relative and a "worthy man," and Naomi trusted Boaz would uphold the law.

Initially, Naomi sent her daughter-in-law, Ruth, to glean in his fields. Then, after seeing how Boaz protected and provided for Ruth in the fields, Naomi sent Ruth to lay at Boaz's feet while he slept.

At the time, this was seen as a request for him to be their redeemer.

But Boaz didn't stop at fulfilling the requirements of the law, he exceeded them. Boaz bought Naomi's family land, fulfilling the law, but then he also married Ruth and had a child with her so Naomi's family line would continue. As Naomi cradled her new grandson, her friends called out a tune far different from Naomi's words that she said upon her return. They said, "Blessed be the Lord, who has not left you this day without a redeemer. He shall be to you a restorer of life and nourisher of your old age."

Naomi, despite her bitterness and despondency, knew her redeemer, and placed her trust in his capable hands. And Boaz was faithful. If this story feels familiar, it should, because Jesus, our Redeemer, repeated this story in our spiritual lives. He is the one who paid our debt of sin by his death on the cross and now calls us his beautiful bride, the ones whom he deeply loves (Isaiah 54:4-8; Revelation 19:7-9).

Like Naomi demonstrated, focusing on the character of God doesn't remove us from this painful world, but it gives us safe harbor through it. So when your life hits a detour filled with disappointment, swim back upstream to the ocean of God's strong character, and saturate yourself in the truth of who God is. He is truly worthy of our trust!

Here are four steps you can take right now:

- Let's see how God defines his character. Look up the verses listed below and note what you learn about God.
  - -Psalm 46
  - -Psalm 96
  - -Ephesians 1:3-10
  - -1 John 4:7-21
- Repeat these to yourself often!
- Declare your surrender at the end of your honest lament.
- Surround yourself with people who will speak truth and hope into your life, like Ruth and Naomi did for each other.

What did you learn about God's character after reviewing the listed verses? Consider writing a prayer of lament in the space provided below.

Building Faith

Sister, I picture you holding this little book and coming to this last page, a page designed to build and encourage your faith. But what does one say to someone who, by the power of God, has already lived as a mighty warrior? You, who have taken the sword of the Spirit and wielded it with power and precision. What does one say to those already walking in truth and life?

I start by saying what I say to my children after every single one of their sporting events: I love watching you play! In the same way, I imagine Jesus smiling upon you with pure joy and thinking, "I love watching you." I don't think he analyzes your every mistake, nor revisits your slip ups and failures. Rather, he is over the moon about you!

Just as a buttercup tilts its face toward the sun, we thrive under the loving warmth of Jesus. Revelation 2 is a clear picture of his priority for the saints who endure. Here, the word of the Lord came to the church in Ephesus, "I know your works, your toil and your patient endurance ... I know you are enduring patiently and bearing up for my name's sake, and you have patiently suffered for me without quitting."

But according to Revelation 2:4, "But I have this complaint against you. You don't love me or each other as you did at first!" Where had the church in Ephesus missed the mark?

During my younger years, I ran a few half marathons. Usually I got bamboozled into it by a few friends, and then I was committed. The honest truth is that I did not love running. But I spent the hours necessary for training because it was a free and healthy workout, one where I could buckle my kids into a stroller.

See the correlation? I was like the church in Ephesus, I had everything but love. So unfortunately, my running hasn't outlasted my kids aging out of the jogging stroller. But what if I loved running? I know a few crazy ladies who do! They keep running. And running. And running.

Let me offer you a gentle nudge, something I'm asking myself even as I write these words. In a spiritual sense, where is your first love? Have you, like the church in Ephesus, toiled and patiently endured, but lost this love? Have you noticed any changes in priorities during the years of your maturing faith?

Take a few moments and talk with God about how you loved him, and what, if anything, has changed?

Think back to your younger relationship with Jesus. Maybe it was in college, or as a high school teen, or young adult. How might you maintain the "love you had at first?"

When we love someone, whether it's the love of a friend or the love of a spouse, spending time with that person becomes a priority. So it is with Jesus. To continue deepening our relationship with Jesus, we must continue to spend time with him. When I look back on my life, my closest friends are the ones I talked to most often.

Here are some suggestions to get you started:

- Find a local church where you can be involved. Spend time serving in the church and connecting with the other members.
- If your church does not offer a women's Bible study, connect with one in your local area. Bible Study Fellowship, Precepts, and Community Bible Studies are all wonderful options.
- Develop rhythms of prayer. These rhythms will change throughout our different seasons of life. For example, when my children were little, I used their naptime to write and pray in my journal; now that my children are all in school, I spend my time walking the dog or cleaning the dishes talking with God. Once you have begun the habit of talking with Jesus throughout your day, you will never go back.

Thankfully, in Jesus, nothing is wasted. Nothing is lost. Not even the years of toil and patient endurance.

But let me leave you with this charge: God is love, and whoever abides in love abides in God, and God abides in him. So beloved, let us love one another, for love is from God, and, first and foremost, let us love the Lord our God with all our heart and with all our soul and with all our mind.

What one or two things will you commit to doing to help build your faith?

ABOUT THE AUTHOR

Julie Bender is a believer, encourager, wifey (formerly widowed), mama, and an oversharer. She strives to be bold in everything: her lipstick and lashes, mistakes and wins, her opinions and her faith.

Her life hasn't been easy.

Julie had a difficult childhood, being a product of two drug-addicted teens who were unable to be parents at the time which left her to be raised by her great-grandmother.

But she's learned to embrace her story. Through her ability to share vulnerably, she found healing and her true self. Her personal mantra is *#beboldandjustbeyou* as she shares her heart, humor, and frequent embarrassing moments.

She hosts *The Julie Bender Show* podcast, co-hosts This *Grit and Grace Life* podcast, and produces a series for wives entitled *#prayingforyourhusbanddaily*. She has been featured on multiple podcasts, including, *Stronger in the Difficult Places*, *Get Your Marriage On!* with Dan Purcell, and a video segment for *HeartofDating.com* with Kait Tomlin.

But remember, she's winging it: motherhood, eyeliner, dinner plans, everything.

Instagram: https://www.instagram.com/thejuliebender/

Facebook: https://www.facebook.com/mrsjuliegraham

YouTube: https://www.youtube.com/@thejuliebender

Website: https://thejuliebender.com/

RESOURCES

Use this QR code to access a free printable companion journal, additional books related to the topic, and more.

Below are additional books in the Smart Living series.

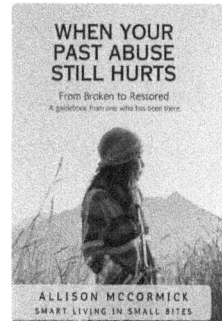

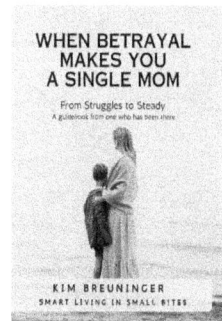

WHEN
MARRIAGE
IS HARD

From Conflict to Connection
A guidebook from one who has been there.

JULIE BENDER
SMART LIVING IN SMALL BITES

WHEN SUICIDE
TOUCHES
YOUR LIFE

From Hurt to Healing
A guidebook from one who has been there.

DARLENE BROCK
SMART LIVING IN SMALL BITES

WHEN YOUR
PAST ABUSE
STILL HURTS

From Broken to Restored
A guidebook from one who has been there.

ALLISON MCCORMICK
SMART LIVING IN SMALL BITES

WHEN ANXIETY
WON'T
LET GO

From Panic to Peace
A guidebook from one who has been there.

CAROLINE BEIDLER, MSW
SMART LIVING IN SMALL BITES

WHEN DATING
AGAIN FEELS
SCARY

From Fearful to Courageous
A guidebook from one who has been there.

MARLYS JOHNSON LAWRY
SMART LIVING IN SMALL BITES

WHEN BETRAYAL
MAKES YOU
A SINGLE MOM

From Struggles to Steady
A guidebook from one who has been there.

KIM BREUNINGER
SMART LIVING IN SMALL BITES

Coming Soon

Other Books

At *Grit and Grace Life*, we strive to bring you great articles every day. Over the years, we've had the honor of sharing practical tips and helpful wisdom with our readers. We couldn't do this without our team of talented writers. Like you, these women are learning to navigate the ups and downs of life with grit and grace.

What you may not know is that many of our writers have dug a bit deeper and written books that can help you (or someone you love) on your journey. Are you ready to change your life?

Use this QR code to access a list of books written by *Grit and Grace Life* writers.

ABOUT GRIT AND GRACE LIFE

Grit and Grace Life is a place for strong women and those who want to be. As a community of women, we have come together to share the life lessons we have learned and the wisdom we have gained. Whether it's through books, videos, social media, podcasts, or on our website, our goal in everything we do is to help women navigate this challenging and wonderful life.

We tackle all things women face, whether big or small, knowing that as we do, we will find strength. We are a collective from every age and every stage of life, here to pass on our stories and the answers we've found through the joys and challenges of our lives. Our driving desire is to provide insights, real-life solutions, hope, and encouragement to all who walk alongside us.

Faith is paramount to who we are and what we do. We have been gently guided in our lives by a God who loves us faithfully and completely. It is in him we find hope and healing. We believe you will, too.

Through all we do at Grit and Grace Life, our prayer is that you would embrace grit and grace as the strongholds of your life, just as we have. And, please, remember this: Grit determines that life challenges won't defeat or define us. Grace gives kindness to ourselves and others, even when it's hard.

www.gritandgracelife.com

This Grit and Grace Life podcast can be heard at:
https://thegritandgraceproject.org/podcast

Follow us on social media:
https://www.facebook.com/ThisGritandGraceLife
https://www.instagram.com/thisgritandgracelife/
https://www.youtube.com/watch?v=mS4O3YC2Ejw

"Marriages, like a garden, take time to grow. But the harvest is rich unto those who patiently and tenderly care for the ground."

—Darlene Schacht

www.ingramcontent.com/pod-product-compliance
Lightning Source LLC
Chambersburg PA
CBHW071454070426
42452CB00039B/1360